T0124493

THE NEXT
RIGHT MOVE

The Next Right Move

Making the Right Career Steps in a Digital Age

J. MARK MUNOZ

AND

STEPHEN KREMPL

UNION BRIDGE BOOKS
An imprint of Wimbledon Publishing Company Limited (WPC)
www.unionbridgebooks.com

This edition first published in UK and USA 2021
by UNION BRIDGE BOOKS
75–76 Blackfriars Road, London SE1 8HA, UK
or PO Box 9779, London SW19 7ZG, UK
and
244 Madison Ave #116, New York, NY 10016, USA

British Library Cataloguing-in-Publication Data
A catalogue record for this book is available from the British Library.

Library of Congress Control Number: 2021939301

ISBN-13: 978-1-78527-990-4 (Hbk)
ISBN-10: 1-78527-990-4 (Hbk)

Cover image: By lkunl/Shutterstock.com

This title is also available as an e-book.

CONTENTS

PROLOGUE

The Next Right Move is a story about three characters who go on a road trip and experience technology, organizations, and work life in 2030.

Through their journey, you will encounter a new job entrant, one in the middle of his career and another who is contemplating on what to do to finish strong.

They all think through key questions and resolve issues individually, from other people or situations encountered along the way. There are exciting learning opportunities relating to how the characters approach, think, and decide on what to do to get ahead in the Corporate America of the future.

We wrote this story because we have our individual passions around artificial intelligence (AI), future trends, and the changing nature of work. The simple story offers unique insights on what scenarios exists, how to manage the challenges, and capitalize on opportunities to achieve career success.

We hope the story will get you to think about what you need to do to prepare for your own future career.

We believe that the featured lessons will help you make the appropriate *right* steps toward your own developmental journey and pathway toward a happy, healthy, and productive life ahead.

1

THE FIRST RIGHT

Lisa Brown, a recent college graduate, yells from the driveway, "I'm almost ready Mom!"

A mix of excitement and sorrow was evident in her voice. She was excited to start her new life in New York. Yet, sad to leave behind family and friends in the small town of Decatur, Illinois, where she grew up.

Ed Brown, Lisa's dad, walked toward her old Ford Fusion, carrying a box containing her clothes. He slid the box on to one side of the trunk and asks, "Is this the last one?"

Lisa shook her head. "I think I have two more."

Ed shook his head. "We're running out of space in the car. You can always bring the rest next time you visit."

In this road trip to New York, Ed will accompany Lisa. The first half of 2030 had not been kind to him. He was laid off in the last quarter of 2029 and simply couldn't find a job. At the age of 55, he was too young to retire, yet too old for the highly competitive job market. More than ten million jobs were lost in 2029, and the available jobs mostly required high technology skills. Although he was a hardworking, affable, and efficient manager, he never found the need to update his technological skills.

He felt like a dinosaur in the digital age. Since he was unemployed, he felt he might as well spend some time with Lisa and help her get settled in her new apartment. He had been disappointed and discouraged during the past months. He believed the trip could be a journey of hope and could help him shake off his depression. He was hoping to have a chance to speak with a few people in the East Coast and explore career or entrepreneurial options. Lisa was starting off on her new career, he wasn't quite ready to end his.

An autonomous car entered the driveway. Ben Johnson, Lisa's 27-year-old boyfriend, stepped out of the car. He waved at Lisa and Ben and pulled out a small suitcase from the car. Ben had decided to join the road trip to New York. His career direction had bothered him lately. It had been four years since he's had a promotion. While he felt lucky to have a job in a depressed economy, he believed he could do better. On the way to New York, he hoped to stop by his company's headquarters in New Jersey. He had set up a meeting with a former office mate, Michael James. Like him, Michael was a Black man with better than average technological skills. Michael climbed up the corporate ladder fairly quickly. He wanted to pick his brains on how he could jumpstart his career. He would love the opportunity to work in the company's head office so that he could be closer to Lisa. Could this road trip change his life?

Ben kissed Lisa, then proceeded to help her with the last two boxes.

They said their goodbyes to Jane, Lisa's mom, and settled in the car.

Like all cars in 2030, the Ford Fusion had an autonomous driving option despite being a few years old.

"Goodbye, Decatur," Lisa said softly. She felt sorry for her hometown. Like many mid-sized, semi-urban cities, jobs have been extremely scarce. America had become obsessed with technology. Highly urbanized cities with the best technological infrastructure and ecosystems were the big winners. The megacities had the best jobs and the highest pay. There could have been a mass exodus in many struggling cities but for the scarcity of housing in the megacities. And, the cost of living was also very high. Without a job in the megacities, you'll end up homeless very quickly. Many tried their luck in the megacities and returned financially ruined and physically and mentally broken. Lisa was excited about her new job in New York. She felt like she had won the lottery. Her family and friends threw a party when they came to hear about her job. Lisa was thankful she graduated with a degree in Cybersecurity. The degree set her apart from many graduates. Though not the most intelligent, she was a hardworker. Her 3.4 GPA was a testament of her work ethic and competence. Yet, she harbored a deep-seated fear about her career in New York. Did she learn enough in school? Would her limited work experience be an impediment? Does she have the grit to make it in a high-stakes, ultra-competitive environment like New York? She tried to shrug off her doubts and fears.

"Please prepare for a *right* turn," Allie the voice behind her autonomous car announced.

Lisa glanced at her side-view mirror. The sign said, "You are now leaving Decatur."

The sign gave her a feeling of finality. This is it. This road trip is the start of her journey. She glanced at Ed and Ben. The two men in her life whom she loved. She knew their fears and disappointments all too well. She understood their despair. Could this trip be the start of a journey for them too? Could the three of them get their career right?

2

GAS STATION

The trio sat quietly in the car. All lost in their own thoughts.

Ed broke the silence. "We probably should fill up the gas tank."

"You're right," Lisa said. "Allie, take us to the nearest gas station, please."

"Yes, Lisa. I'll make this *right* turn and we should be on our way," the car responded.

Allie parked next to the gas pump and automatically opened the gas tank.

"Good morning, Ms. Brown. I am Gary, your robo-attendant. Shall I fill up the tank?"

"Yes, please," Lisa said.

"Good morning as well, Mr. Brown and Mr. Johnson." Gary automatically extended the hose to the gas tank to fill up. "Ms. Brown, we have a special discount today on coffee and organic snacks. Should I pre-order some for you?"

"No, thank you, Gary," Lisa responded, smiling.

"Mr. Brown, we have veggie hotdogs. Would that be of interest?"

"No, thanks," Ed answered.

"Mr. Johnson, would you like natural apple-flavored vitamin water?"

"Not today, Gary. Thank you," Ben chuckled. "You know me well."

"I try, Sir. Ms. Brown, I noticed your front driver's side tire pressure is somewhat low—should I add air to it?"

"Yes, please."

"Right away. It's my pleasure," Gary said. "Would you want me to clean your car windows?"

"No, thank you."

"Your total bill is $30. Would you like to pay by cash, card account, or cryptocurrency?"

"Card account, please."

Lisa raised her right hand so that Gary could digitally read and process her implanted microchip at the base of the back of her hand.

"Bill processed. Thank you, everyone. Please come again and do have a good day," Gary said, cheerfully. "By the way, just about six miles into the highway there's just been a road mishap. You may want to alter your course. Do drive safely."

"Thank you, Gary," Lisa said, smiling.

"Quite a service they deliver," Ed commented. "I remember the time when there were humans manning the gas pumps. Those were the days. The service was not as quick and efficient, but it was real human-to-human interaction. It's just not the same."

"So you think the robots do a better job, Dad?" Lisa asked.

"They are far more efficient. They are programmed to be that way. But the human touch is missing. Human beings with all their faults still understand other human beings better," Ed offered.

Ben nodded. "I agree, the problem is that companies are driven by efficiency and profitability. At the end of the day, if robots provide a better bottom line, they become the better choice."

"The problem," Lisa added, "is that Corporate America has become so callous. How many people do we know have lost their jobs to bots, robots, and avatars? I feel it's almost like we're going on a war against the robots. A do-or-die battle, a fierce competition in the battle for efficiency."

The conversation was quite painful for Ed to hear. He thought about his past job and how he neglected skill-upgrading opportunities. He didn't bother too much about efficiency. He was one of those who truly believed it's all about relationships. Work gets done by the sheer strength of human interaction.

Ed decided to speak up. "As you know, I am one of those losers in this so-called battle for efficiency. I am one of millions. I knew technology was important. I never thought it would be so important that it would wipe out millions of human jobs in a span of few years. I wish I had prepared myself better for this battle. I should have enlisted in the technology-training programs that my company offered. Maybe I should have taken online classes in arti-ficial intelligence and automation to update my skills. This way, I could have stayed valuable to the company."

Lisa could sense Ed's despair. "It's never too late, Dad."

Ed nodded. "It's just that everything seemed to have happened so quickly. I saw our company automating a little here, and a little there. I never expected it to converge all together at once. It was as if humans lost the efficiency battle here, and then there, and before you knew it, the whole company became automated and the humans—at least in our company—lost the entire war."

Ben empathized. "The same thing happened in our company, Ed. I was fortunate to have a strong tech foundation in my college years. It really helped me keep my job. I'm glad I had the foresight to take all skill-upgrading programs I could lay my hands on—both in the company and through online education. There is also some benefit in leveraging emotional quotient (EQ) and finding synergies between humans and machines. At the end of the day, in our ten-person department, only two of us remain now. I guess I survived the efficiency battle with machines. The problem is, the war is not over."

"It looks like it's going to be a long battle . . . a big war," Ed said. "It now seems that the much-dreaded World War III is not going to be between countries and humans. It will be between humans and machines. It won't be in the battlefield. It will be closer to home—in boardrooms, in offices, in factories. By not participating in technological skills-upgrading programs, it's like I went to battle with a pen knife and my opponents had grenade launchers and bazookas."

Ben smiled. "Interesting analogy. I guess as a soldier of technology, learning new skills will be like building an artillery for the war against machines. These training programs are not just fancy knowledge, they are survival tools!"

Ed shook his head and said solemnly, "I really wish I knew that before."

Lisa looked at her dad, sadly. She had witnessed his sorrow and frustration in the past months. He had applied for thousands of jobs and never received a single call. Not even a single interview. She made an effort to console him, "Don't worry, Dad. Perhaps there's a way to converge your existing skill sets with a technological tool. Perhaps there's a niche career opportunity for you."

He looked at her gratefully. "Perhaps. I hope so, dearie."

The conversation they just had worried Lisa. "As I embark on my career, am I immediately dragged into this battle or war with machines? Do I have what it takes to succeed? What should I do to be well equipped to win?" she wondered.

One thought came to mind. She would have a fighting chance if she continually upgraded her skill sets to achieve the highest level of efficiency.

Right Turn Lesson # 1

Employees need to upgrade their skills and pursue lifelong learning to keep their jobs.

Technology Roadmap

Blockchain is a shared and immutable ledger designed to note transactions, build trust, and monitor assets. It is the framework for many cryptocurrencies. The blockchain devices market is expected to surpass $23.5 billion by 2030. Blockchain is projected to make an impact on industries such as banking, real estate, healthcare, education, retail, energy management, hedge funds, stock trading, insurance, and Internet advertising among many others. The Stanford Center for Blockchain Research offers useful information and resources on this technology.

For more information go to the epilogue.

3

RESTAURANT

The trio had been on the road for several hours. They felt a degree of excitement about new career prospects and opportunities. Yet, they also harbored a fear of the unknown and the prospects of failure.

While the drive was physically comfortable with Allie's autonomous driving, it was mentally and emotionally challenging.

"Please prepare for a *right* turn," Allie announced.

Ben's train of thought was interrupted, "Ok, I think I'm about ready for lunch."

Lisa smiled. "Good idea. Any preference?"

Ed squirmed. "How about the nearest one? I really need to use the restroom."

Lisa nodded. "Ok, Allie please take us to the nearest restaurant."

"Yes, Lisa. We're on our way. We should be there in about 7 minutes," the car announced.

Ed grumbled. "Can we make it sooner? I really need to use the restroom."

"Yes, Mr. Brown. I'll get you to the restaurant entrance in 4 minutes and 50 seconds," the car said.

"Thank you, Ellie."

"You're welcome. By the way, its Allie. Just relax, we'll be there soon."

In perfect timing, the car parked right by the entrance. Ed rushed to the restroom.

A virtual human reality or avatar welcomed them.

"Good afternoon. My name is Lanie, and I'm your guest relations avatar and server. Welcome to Stelarz."

"Thank you, Lanie. A table for three, please," Lisa said. She was struck by the number of avatars standing by. There were about 20 of them in total at the restaurant. All stood ready to serve the guests and provide a personalized dining experience. They all looked similar to Lanie, but they had different skin, eye, and hair color. She wondered whether they had different accents as well.

Ed caught up with Tom and Lisa.

"Follow me, please," Lanie said, as she led the way to the table. "Please have a seat."

She readjusted the height of the table to provide optimal comfort for the trio.

"May I get you something to drink?"

"Just water for me," Lisa responded.

"Same here," Ed said.

"Vitamin mineral water, natural apple flavor, please," Ben said.

"Would you want that in green apple or red apple flavor, Mr. Johnson?"

"Oh," Ben answered. "Sorry, red please."

"Thank you, Mr. Johnson."

Within 10 seconds, the drinks were delivered by a robo-server.

This quick service never ceased to amaze Ed. He remembered how much longer the orders took to come when humans did the serving. He spotted several robo-cooks in the kitchen, all doing methodical and precision cooking. It was consistent work with no errors.

Lanie smiled at the trio. "Your digital menu is viewable in front of you on the table. Please feel free to simply touch your selection. As you can see, we have several specials for the day, today. Your biometrics statistics indicate that Ms. Brown, you have 1,526 recommended calories remaining for the day. Mr. Brown, you have 1,925, and Mr. Johnson, you have 2,277. The meal calorie count is shown beside the item photo. Just touch your selection on the table screen, and your order will be served in approximately 1 minute. Enjoy your meal!"

They touched the table screen for their orders, and true enough their ordered food arrived in exactly 1 minute.

As they started eating, Ed asked, "Did you notice that aside from the customers there's only one human in the restaurant? The rest are avatars and robots."

Ben nodded. "I did notice it. He must be the restaurant manager. Restaurants used to have several humans, and then, one by one the human jobs disappeared. I wonder what skill sets the manager had that allowed him to be the last man standing?"

Lisa wiped her mouth and said, "I'm sure he has some solid tech skills that made him stand out from the rest. He probably had some background in artificial intelligence and automation. It looks like he'd play an active role in programing and monitoring the robots and avatars."

Ben added, "And trouble shoot too when things go wrong."

Ed looked at the manager closely for a minute and said, "He probably would have to know something about food and beverage as well."

Lisa was surprised. "Wow, what a unique set of skills—food, beverage, AI, automation, and management."

"Quite a world we're living in," Ed said. "It looks like in this highly competitive job market, workers really need to acquire a combination of unique skills that will really set them apart."

"Not only do they need to make themselves stand out in the job market," Ben added, "they need to also focus on where they can add real value. In the case of the restaurant manager, his unique blend of skills relating to food and beverage and the digital world really gave him an upper hand. In the company he works for, he has become an MVP—Most Valued Person."

Ed was pensive for a moment. "It looks like all employees in the digital age have to aspire to be that MVP. They have to train hard and work hard. Quite like gaining the stature of a Most Valuable Player in the world of sports."

"It's somewhat different from the sports world though," Ben added. "In sports, typically one MVP is chosen per season. In business, there could be several. But you need to obtain that status and stay very useful and relevant to your company."

"Yes," Ed agreed. "It could be more challenging in business because you're constantly competing with several other MVPs. One misstep and you could be out of a job."

The conversation suddenly saddened Ben. "I guess my lack of promotion in my job means I don't have an MVP status."

Ed looked at him, solemnly. "I lost my MVP status many years ago. I guess I'll need to find a way to regain it—maybe in a new company or my own business."

Ben nodded. "I'll have to regain my MVP status too, and soon!"

Lisa pondered on what Ed and Ben talked about. She's just about to embark on a new career. She wondered how many MVPs she'll be up against. She made a mental note to ask her supervisor exactly what skills are necessary for her to excel in her job. She too needs to become an MVP.

Right Turn Lesson # 2

Competition will be tough. Employees need to differentiate their skills and focus on where they can truly add value.

Technology Roadmap

Augmented reality refers to an interactive experience of a real-world setting wherein objects in the real world are enhanced using computers. Mobile-augmented reality market is expected to reach $24 billion by 2030. Industries that would be impacted by this technology include retail, military and defense, events and conferences, marketing and advertising, law enforcement, recruiting and talent management, manufacturing and logistics, customer service, healthcare and medicine, journalism, film and entertainment, and agriculture among many others. The MIT Media Lab highlights cutting-edge information-augmented reality technology.

For more information go to the epilogue.

4

HOTEL

The trio stepped out of the restaurant, and Allie had the autonomous car waiting right by the front door.

As they passed through the major highway, featured technological breakthroughs and innovative products flashed in digital, interactive signages.

Tracking devices were everywhere. There was constant monitoring of vehicle speed, car problems, and all suspicious activities. It was a fully interconnected world where physical products were linked with the digital.

Privacy had become a thing of the past. Government policies and bills were passed several years ago and provided a clear choice and verdict. The global community had decided. Full digital connectivity was more preferable than privacy.

Individuals, companies, and governments at first struggled with this new notion. It took time to get used to. It took time to be completely transparent to the entire world and to have all machines know everything about a person. It took only a split second for a machine to gather and analyze information pertaining to a person's biographical and health profile, intelligence, desires and interests, family and friends, purchase behavior, and everything conceivable. It was total and complete transparency for everyone.

Of course, not everyone wanted it this way. Not everyone wanted a microchip implanted at the back of one hand that constantly tracked their activities and biometrics. The upside is that you could have an ambulance with robo-responders in the front door of your house before you even knew you had a heart attack. Grocery was delivered to your doorstep before you even knew you'd run out of supplies. Robo-cops could be in your home before you even knew there was an intruder.

Allie spoke, suddenly. "Mr. Brown, your blood pressure is slightly elevated. I suggest you take your medication."

It caught Ed by surprise. "I see, thank you, Allie." He had forgotten to take his medication and was pleased with the reminder.

Ed looked at the microchip at the back of his hand. He was one of those who never wanted one. He was definitely one of the last adapters. He hated the idea of being constantly monitored. Ultimately, he had no choice. The company he worked for made it a policy. The US and all other governments around the world made it a law.

Of course, there were dissenters—people who couldn't live with a microchip in their body. They ripped it from their hands and lived a life off the grid or underground. Some became homeless, others became beggars, still others became survivalists or homesteaders. All of them were hiding from the law all of the time.

Ed had the chip to be thankful for. With mass unemployment and large number of dissenters, crime was on the rise. One night, a dissenter entered his home and attempted to steal food. The robo-cops arrived quickly and neutralized the dissenter. The robo-cops may have saved his life.

Ed caught Lisa yawning. It was already 9:00 p.m. It had been a long day.

"Should we find a hotel and call it a day?" Ed suggested.

"I agree. Allie, can you take us to the nearest hotel, please?"

"Absolutely, Lisa. Please prepare for a *right* turn."

Allie parked the car right by the hotel entrance. The trio disembarked with their travel bags in tow.

A robo-bellman welcomed them. "Good evening, my name is Bob and I'm your robo-bellman. Welcome to Gallarz, Mr. and Ms. Brown and Mr. Johnson. Complimentary beverages and organic snacks are available next to the lobby. Mr. and Ms. Brown, the bottled water is chilled. Mr. Johnson, the vitamin mineral water, natural red apple flavor is ready."

"Thank you, Bob," Lisa said.

As they moved toward the lobby and front desk, the ambiance changed based on their collective preferences—type of background music, lighting, temperature, art decor, and even the scent.

"Good evening, Mr. and Ms. Brown and Mr. Johnson. I'm Jill. Welcome to Gallarz," the robo-clerk said. "Two rooms or three?"

"Two rooms, please. Ben and I will share," Lisa answered.

"Excellent! Your rooms are ready. Would you prefer to pay in cash, card account, or cryptocurrency?" Jill asked, politely.

"Card account. You can charge both rooms to me," Ed offered.

Lisa argued. "You don't have to, Dad. We can take care of it."

"I insist. It's the least I can do to help."

"Thanks, Dad."

"Hey, you're welcome, dearie."

Jill did an auto scan on the trio to confirm room specifications and ambiance. By the time they got to the room everything was to their exact historical preferences—music, lighting, room temperature, art, scent—and even water temperature.

"Mr. Brown, your biometrics show that your back is sore. Would you want me to send over a robo-masseuse?"

"Not tonight, thank you though."

"Would you want a virtual casino set up in your room?"

"Huh?" Ed responded, surprised and confused.

"My files show that you like gambling," Jill said.

"What? No!" Ed said, emphatically, red-faced.

Ed looked at Lisa and Ben, sheepishly. "She must have picked up something from my historical records. I may have accidentally stumbled into an online gaming site once."

Ben looked at Ed suspiciously, and in a teasing manner asked, "Accidentally?"

Lisa looked at her dad, surprised. "Dad?!"

"I swear! It was a long time ago. A digital accident, maybe this is just a computer glitch. Definitely! A computer glitch. I am not a gambler!" Ed said, defensively.

Ed looked at Jill. "No, definitely no gambling tonight."

Ben and Lisa looked at Ed, suspiciously.

"As you please, Mr. Brown. Is there anything else I can do for all of you?"

Lisa looked at Jill. It never ceased to amaze her how close to human the robo-clerk looked like. Yet, they had a lot to learn about human nature and what an appropriate conversation should be like. Lisa spoke for the group, "I think we're all good, thank you."

The trio proceeded toward the lobby elevator.

"I've not seen a single human so far. Have you?" Ed asked, as the elevator door opened.

"Nope," Ben answered. Right after he spoke, a house-keeping lady stepped in the elevator.

"Good evening," she said. Fumbling with two tech devices and their augmented realities, she struggled to control the devices. An avatar kept appearing and disappearing from her screen. An assortment of avatar images were projected to the side and the top of the elevator. Scrambled avatar digital voices could be heard.

"I'm so sorry," the housekeeper said, apologetically. "I can't seem to get used to these devices. They arrived last week. I took the training, but can't seem to get it right."

Ed looked at her, sympathetically. "Happens to me all the time with all this new tech gadgets."

She smiled, and continued tampering with the devices. The words "computer error, please try again" could be heard from one device.

Lisa wanted to help her, but was unsure as to what exactly she was supposed to do.

The trio empathized with her. They have been in similar situations. It was not easy staying abreast with all the technology that were being developed.

Ed decided to ask a question. "I'm sorry, just out of curiosity, what tech degree is needed for housekeepers, nowadays?"

The housekeeper looked at him and answered. "No tech degree needed for our jobs, just several upskilling programs. Too many, I think. I attend some form of training once a week. There are so many gadgets to learn about. I don't think I'm well prepared for all this new technology, but I need to adapt in order to keep my job."

Ed offered a compliment. "You must be a very good housekeeper."

"Yes," the housekeeper whispered. "I'm very skilled in housekeeping, but not at all good in technology. I'm so thankful they are still letting me keep my job. I'm not sure for how long."

The elevator door opened.

"Well, good luck to you then," Ed said.

"Thank you," the housekeeper said. "Do have a good night."

The trio proceeded to their technology-enhanced bedrooms.

Lisa felt so sorry for the housekeeper. All these new tech gadgets were way above her head. Even with a tech degree of her own, she often struggled. There were just too many gadgets and too fast. Lisa came upon another realization. Employees need to be prepared to make technology an integral part of their work lives. They need to promptly adapt to rapid technological changes unfolding before their eyes.

Right Turn Lesson # 3

Many new technological gadgets and tools will emerge. Employees need to learn to embrace technology quickly.

Technology Roadmap

Robotics refers to the interface between computer science and engineering leading to the creation of intelligent machines that assist humans and enhance workplace productivity. The global autonomous mobile robots market is expected to reach $220 billion in 2030. Key industries that will be impacted by this technology include healthcare, agriculture, food preparation, manufacturing, transportation, military, and law enforcement among many others. McKinsey Report titled "Industrial Robotics: Insights into the Sector's Future Growth Dynamics" is available on the web and provides useful information on this technology.

For more information go to the epilogue.

5

HOUSE

The trio left the hotel early in the morning. They hoped to get to Washington, DC, sometime in the afternoon to visit Ed's sister-in-law and Lisa's aunt, Cindy Edwards.

Cindy was a nurse who opted to retire early. Her husband Jim was a technology consultant who helped build artificial intelligence (AI) and Internet of Things (IoT) systems. Cindy decided on a career shift in order to help Jim with his consulting practice. The duo built a booming business that provided technological products to the healthcare industry.

By mid-afternoon, Allie made a *right* turn to enter the long and oversized driveway of a large and elegant-looking house.

The trio disembarked from the car, and Ed proceeded to ring the doorbell.

An avatar welcomed them to Cindy's home. "Good afternoon, I'm Mike, the butler. Welcome Mr. and Ms. Brown and Mr. Johnson. Please follow me. Ms. Edwards will join you shortly."

Mike led them to the living room and said, "Please make yourselves comfortable. I'll have water, tea, and snacks brought in shortly. I'm sorry we don't have the vitamin mineral water, natural red apple flavor, Mr. Johnson. Can I get you anything else?"

Ben was in disbelief. Every machine seemed to know everything about him, including an avatar in Washington, DC. "Water would be fine, thank you," he said, trying his best to conceal his frustration. He couldn't quite point a finger on what bothered him—could it be the complete and absolute loss of privacy?

As Mike left, Lisa let her eyes wander around Aunt Cindy's house. It was elegantly designed. It has all the trappings of what is known as a smart home. She remembered discussing it in class. But, she had actually never seen one in her life. In this type of home, the temperature and lighting were automatically controlled based on the homeowner's desired settings. Everything was controlled via voice. You could speak to your television, your refrigerator, your oven, and even your vacuum cleaner. Your refrigerator was linked to your grocery store, which automatically tracked inventory and ordered a delivery from the grocer when supply ran low. This type of home typically had a virtual fashion designer in your bedroom. Using AI, the designer scanned your physique and mood and offered attire recommendations. The designer even made purchase suggestions based on your preferred style and past purchasing history. All you had to do was say "yes" or "no." Desired products were delivered to your doorstep within a few hours. In the bathroom, the shower and toilet operated entirely based on your specifications. All appliances had built-in intelligence and were completely interconnected.

In this type of smart home, the family room was the headquarters. Augmented-reality screens allowed you to connect with any family member or any person in the world instantaneously by voice command. Any question you asked would be answered in seconds. Your entertainment options got projected on the screen the moment you stepped in—including news, sporting events, and concerts anywhere in the world.

Lisa was very excited to have had the chance to see one. She looked forward to telling her friends about it.

Cindy stepped in the room. "Sorry, it took a while. I had some business to wrap up. It's such a pleasure to see you! Thank you so much, for visiting!" She gave everyone a hearty kiss and a hug.

"You have such a lovely place, Cindy," Ed commented, admiringly.

"I would have preferred a simpler house. Jim is fascinated with technology and wants to have all the tech trappings. Wait, I forgot something. Let me go get my P-I-N-S."

The trio was surprised. They wondered. "Why on earth would she need pins?"

Cindy came back to the room with a pen-like object. "This is our P-I-N-S—Personal Internet of Things Networked System. This small contraption is actually the brain of the house. It connects all appliances together and with the outside world. This also controls Mike, our avatar butler, who brings us what we ask for. I need it with me all the time. It's like my magic wand."

Lisa was amazed. "That's quite impressive, Aunt Cindy. Do all appliances connect together well?"

"Are there no computer glitches?" Tom asked, giving Ed a side glance.

"None, whatsoever," Cindy answered. "Everything operates perfectly like clockwork. We just have to be extra cautious about a potential cyberattack. If our system gets hacked, we can become hostages in our own home. At times, we have to reset systems when there's power failure, but that rarely happens."

Ed was impressed. "How's your business going?"

Cindy nodded. "It's doing very well. Our consulting practice has shifted our focus to symbiotic computing—helping employees work in a synergistic way with machines. In hospitals, humans are sometimes threatened by the presence of machines because of their intelligence, efficiency, and well . . . they replace jobs. On the other hand, machines lack sophistication in their communication and miss the human sensitivity angle. Misunderstandings and conflicts between humans and machines are frequent in a hospital setting. In some instances, it diminishes proper patient care. Our consulting company helps organizations find operational harmony. Humans and machines need each other and we're helping hospitals across the country make this interaction as smooth and seamless as possible."

"That's great to hear," Ed said.

Cindy's eyes lit up. "By the way, Jim and I had been exploring the idea of transferring our business model to the factory setting. Didn't you run a factory in the past?"

Ed nodded. "Yes, I did. I worked in a factory for twenty years."

"Would you be interested in helping me and Jim develop the factory symbiotic computing model?"

Ed smiled. "I'd love to. Unfortunately, I know factory work well but know very little about technology."

Cindy was persistent. "Don't worry. That's where Jim comes in. He knows a lot about technology but nothing about factory operations. I think you'd make a great team.

We can create a new company spinoff for this initiative, and you'd be our partner and co-founder."

Ed was excited. "I'd be happy to explore. Thank you, for the offer."

"No, thank you! Jim and I have been wanting to do this for sometime now. I'm so glad you visited, and we had the chance to talk about it," Cindy said.

Ed's heart was racing. It was a brilliant idea. This could be the break he'd been looking for. He was too young to retire. He'd like to spend the next 10 to 20 years leveraging his skills and continue being an active contributor to society. This initiative would not only be financially rewarding, it would help him make a real difference in the business world.

Cindy insisted that the trio stay for dinner and spend the night in her home. It would be an opportunity time for Ed and Jim to further discuss their planned venture.

Lisa loved the idea of spending the night there. She would get to actually experience living in a smart home. She also never got to spend much time with her aunt, this was a great bonding moment. With her new job in New York, she could now visit her aunt more frequently.

Cindy enjoyed giving the trio a tour of the house. As she walked them to the guest room, she offered a suggestion for Lisa. "By the way, when you get to New York, you may want to visit your cousin, Jane. Her workplace has cutting-edge career building initiatives. She could give you some valuable advice."

"I definitely will. I also haven't seen her in years. It would be nice to touch base again. Thanks for the suggestion, Aunt Cindy."

"Not at all," Cindy answered. "Rest well. I'll see you in the morning."

As Lisa unpacked her clothes, she recalled the conversation that afternoon. Symbiotic computing—what an interesting concept and one that's very much needed in the digital age. It was evident that Ed's conversation with Jim during and after dinner went well. Both men were excited about the business possibilities and planned for a way forward. Lisa decided to learn more about symbiotic computing. It could be very useful in her new job.

Right Turn Lesson # 4

There will be machines and robots in the workplace. Employees need to learn to work hand in hand with machines and practice symbiotic computing.

Technology Roadmap

Artificial Intelligence is intelligence provided by machines that mimic human cognitive functions like learning and solving problems. According to a PwC report, AI is estimated to contribute $15.7 trillion to the global economy by 2030. Industries that will be impacted by this technology include cybersecurity, manufacturing, healthcare, education, construction, retail, fashion, business intelligence, supply chain planning, and city planning among many others. A PwC Report titled, "Sizing the Prize: PwC's Global Artificial Intelligence Study: Exploiting the AI Revolution" is available on the web and is a useful resource for understanding this technology.

For more information go to the epilogue.

6

GOVERNMENT

After breakfast, the trio stepped out of the house and prepared to head onward to New York. Cindy and Jim stood at their front door to say their goodbyes.

As the trio proceeded to the car, Ed turned back and said, "I will certainly follow up with both of you on your offer after I return from New York, if that's ok with you."

Jim gave a thumbs-up and said, "Don't take forever. It sounds like we can have a real chance for an interesting venture here."

"Yes, I will," said Ed.

With a final wave, the three of them got into the car and headed off. In the car, they reflected on the impressive use of technology in the house. When you are able to incorporate technology well and humans co-exist with machines properly, everything can work out beautifully.

As they headed out of the neighborhood, Allie announced, "Please prepare for a *right* turn."

The trio planned to make a short stop to meet Ed's college hostel roommate Phil Sanchez. Ed had not seen Phil in 10 years. His last visit was during a trip they took to DC with the family.

Phil was a year younger than him, but even in college he was encouraged by his parents to take up a degree in technology. He finally graduated with a degree in engineering with specialization in AI. It worked out well for him because he was one of the few minorities who had that specialization and technical know-how. He went up the ladder to become the Assistant Secretary of the Department of Artificial Intelligence and Automation (DOAIA).

They reached the outskirts of DC in good time and arrived at the DOAIA building right before their scheduled 11:00 a.m. meeting.

As they entered the garage facility, they passed through a scanner. Within seconds, the car's number plate was recognized on the screen and each person's biometric chip was recorded. The signboard displayed the lot number assigned to them.

Ed was fascinated and said, "I love this efficiency. It sure beats driving around looking for an open spot."

Ben chimed in. "I actually read that there are self-parking garages now, which literally take over when you drive up. A conveyor takes your car to the lot and brings it back to you when you are done."

Lisa surveyed the busy parking lot. "Well, I guess they haven't got that down here yet. But, I could see that all the parked autonomous cars are quietly humming and talking to each other and waiting for the owners to call."

"We certainly do that and more," Allie said, navigating the car skillfully.

"You do such a great job, Allie," Lisa complimented.

"Thank you, Lisa, and you can always trust me," Allie assured her.

The trio exited the car and walked to the nearest door. A robo-guard reconfirmed their meeting.

"I see you're here to meet with Assistant Secretary Sanchez," The robo-guard stated in a formal and distant manner.

"Yes," Jim answered. He wondered whether the robo-guard's programmer created him with a bias that public servants had to be civil and detached. He pondered on the future of government. Could there be robo-politicians too? Do machines get to vote?

"Secretary Sanchez is ready. Please follow the blue line to the elevators," the robo-guard said, in a plain and unemotional tone.

The trio proceeded to the lobby. Along with other guests, they walked through a glass chamber and stood for five seconds. The chamber functioned as a metal detector, biometric reader, and sanitizer. In a few seconds, your historical records get processed, security threat assessed, and all body contaminants such as viruses and microbes get instantly eliminated.

Lisa was astonished. "Wow, what an experience. I didn't really feel a thing."

Ben agreed. "Yes. They have them in all hospitals and many offices these days. It's to beef up security and ensure that all harmful contaminants are removed."

"You know, we probably need one in all homes," Ed added.

"Maybe you and Jim can make that happen through your new company," Lisa said.

They all laughed. Ed thought to himself, "I am starting to like this trip, really looking forward to seeing Phil."

On the other side of the scanner, they were met by an avatar who escorted them to the meeting room.

Ed reminisced. "While in college, Phil always talked about being of service to people and the country; especially since the country provided his foreign-born parents with the opportunity to pursue the American Dream. America gave Phil the platform to build on his passion and talent in a grand way. He opted to use this platform to make a difference in the lives of American people."

"Ed Brown!" Phil Sanchez' booming voice jolted everyone. "It has been a very long time . . . too long." The two men give each other a big hug.

"How are you doing?" Phil asked, enthusiastically.

Ed smiled. "I am doing great. By the way, I want you to meet Lisa and her boyfriend, Ben Johnson."

"It's a pleasure to meet you, Ben. Lisa, the last time I saw you, you were in Middle School," Phil said. "What brings you to DC?"

"We're actually on our way to New York to accompany Lisa on her new job. Ben is taking the opportunity to meet up with people at his company headquarters in New Jersey. We thought we'd stop by and say hello."

"I'm so glad you did!"

They spent a few minutes catching up, discussing college mates, and then Phil's transition to DC.

"Phil, you've been in the thick of AI and automation for a while now. The new technology transformed society in a grand way. How has it changed the way government works?"

"Well, let me show you," Phil said, proudly.

Phil walked over to a wall panel and placed his hand over it. Instantly, like magic, three screens appeared from behind the wall. He proceeded, "Let me explain what AI has done for us in government."

"In real-time, we have these three dashboards that indicate exactly what our citizens are thinking. As you can see on the map, it shows data by state as well as the nation overall. Through this, we immediately know—the local issues, concerns, and needs." He paused to make sure the trio understood. "The second screen lists the resources available for each location and how fast they can be obtained and mobilized. The third screen rolls all those up together in the state and country level. He touched the virtual screen. "This helps us here in DC to focus on the biggest needs and priorities. It helps us plan, monitor, and assess where we should deploy resources. Since we used this system, productivity increased by 50 percent and cost was reduced by 35 percent. We're also able to make decisions much faster and better respond to the needs of citizens."

Ed was astounded. "That . . . is truly impressive."

'We're not done," Phil continued. "The state government can also link into the same system and view their own data by counties, cities, towns, villages, and even districts—school districts, water districts, park districts, airport districts—you name it."

"And your organization created all this?" Ed asked.

Phil nodded. "It was one of the first things that the first secretary of DOAIA was tasked to do. We finally developed a system that is truly useful in managing the country more effectively. It helped preserve the country's dwindling financial resources."

Lisa listened, curiously. "Given there's a lot of dissent in politics, did everyone agree to proceeding with this?"

Phil shook his head. "No . . . No . . . Lisa. You will soon find out in your new job that coming up with an idea is the easy part. Getting everyone onboard, getting them to provide their inputs, and making them feel that the system will not be compromised or abused is the bigger hurdle."

Phil closed his hand and the virtual screen display disappeared. "Think about it this way. Technology can be built but there are no switches or chips to use where human beings' feelings and beliefs are concerned. So, you have to understand both the technology and human behavior."

"My boss once said that in order to succeed and be effective in the work world, you need both," Ben added.

Phil agreed. "That is absolutely true."

Ben chimed in again. "It looks like the explosion of AI and automation will be daunting to many. But, everyone needs to overcome and manage that fear of technology."

Phil was pensive for a minute, then spoke. "You know it was not easy rolling out this system nationwide. Officials across all government levels felt intimidated by the new system. They were concerned that they didn't have the right skills. They feared that they couldn't make it work right."

"How did you make it work?"

"It took some time. We had to educate them. Helped them overcome the fear by taking baby tech steps. We introduced small technological progress one at a time. Ultimately, the entire system got linked together and everyone loved it!"

Ed chimed in. "We all are exposed to all kinds of technology all the time. We need to have a mindshift and do away with technological insecurity and fear. For the most part we are comfortable with our phones, our computers, our cars, our buildings, our doctor's offices. We just need to look at emerging technologies in a new way and be prepared to face them head on, gradually ... a step at a time."

Lisa was amused to see the change in her dad. "Wow, look who's talking these days."

Right Turn Lesson # 5

Emerging technologies will be daunting to many. Employees need to overcome technological insecurity and fear by changing their attitude and taking gradual steps toward progress.

Technology Roadmap

Quantum Computing is a computing approach that uses computer technology from principles derived from quantum theory and examines material and energy behavior within the atomic and subatomic realm. The quantum computing market is projected to reach $64,988 million by 2030 according to a Research and Markets report. Industries that could benefit from this technology include aviation, data analytics, forecasting, medical research, and autonomous cars among many others. A McKinsey Report titled, "A Game Plan for Quantum Computing" is available over the web and provides useful information on this technology.

For more information go to the epilogue.

7

OFFICE

After the stopover in DC, at the DOAIA, the trio headed to New York to meet with Janice Edwards, Lisa's cousin, who spent five years in a small digital marketing company.

As they head out of DC on Highway 195, headed to New York, Allie announced that there is a traffic accident 10 miles ahead and wanted to know if Lisa wished to take an alternate route via Highway 50 to 30 to get to New York.

"Yes definitely," Lisa said, grateful for the notification.

"Great! I'll take the next *right* turn to Highway 50."

On the way, Ben thought about how far the US government had gone, and how they finally got things right for the people they were supposed to serve.

He pondered. "Phil was such a success, and what he accomplished made a difference on the lives of many. Even as a minority, he was able to overcome racial challenges and limitations and managed to get to rise to the top. Phil's story inspired him since he was a minority too. He vowed to put in his best effort to succeed. He would love a promotion or, perhaps, find a new career track. He yearned for a change. He dreamt that one day he could start a family with Lisa. What should he do? How could he do it?" His thought was abruptly interrupted.

"Lisa, what time did you say we were supposed to meet up with Janice?" Ed asked.

"I just asked Allie to send her our latest ETA based on our new route. It should take us another 3 hours and 30 minutes," Lisa replied.

They arrived at Janice's office building at 4:00 p.m. Allie parked across the street and informed the trio that they should be able to get to the lobby within 3 minutes.

Janice was already at the entrance of the building. She waved at them, excitedly.

"Lisa, it's so good to see you," Janice said, as she gave Lisa a hug.

She looked at Ed, and hugged him too. "How have you been, Uncle Ed?"

"Oh, I've been well. Thank you, Janice," Ed said happily.

Lisa reached out to Ben's arm. "Janice, this is my friend, Ben."

"It's nice to meet you, Ben. Do you guys want to come up and see the office?" Janice asked.

"Sure," Ed responded.

The building was a six-story green building. Each tenant had their own elevators to get to their floors for increased security and protection against any viral contamination. Despite in-roads in technology, society in general continually had to worry about people and nature. Cyber-theft and the emergence of unpredictable and frequent pandemics led to numerous challenges. Companies—both big and small—had to invest heavily on safety and security and take precautions.

Janice's office was on the sixth floor. They passed through the growingly common security and biometric scanner disinfectant machine.

The robo-secretary greeted them and told Janice that there was a security breach she needed to take care of first. Janice excused herself and the robo-secretary led them to the meeting room.

The meeting room overlooked the Hudson River. As they all looked over the water, they could see a portion of the New York skyline from a distance.

The view was breathtaking. Lisa said, excitedly. "That's going to be home soon!"

Ed joined her in admiring the view. "I am so proud of you, Lisa. This is a major accomplishment. Considering the state of the job market, this is truly amazing."

Lisa looked worried. "Dad, I'm somewhat worried. I'm not sure I've learned enough in college to make it in a place like New York. There could be many other skills I'm missing. There are so many new technology tools that are introduced almost on a daily basis."

Ben interjected. "You'll do fine, Lisa. You've mastered similar tech programs and did very well on your cybersecurity projects. You have a sound foundation to succeed."

Lisa was about to respond when Janice popped into the room. She apologized for the delay. As office manager, she had to respond to workplace crisis, immediately. Especially if it related to security threats.

As the robo-secretary sets up everyone's favorite drinks, they reminisced old times and discussed new developments in the family. Through augmented reality, family images appeared on a virtual screen.

Janice was curious about Lisa's new job. "Who are you going to be working for, Lisa?"

"I am joining SpaceZ Travel Group. I'll be with the cybersecurity team," Lisa said.

Janice was impressed. "Wow, that's an amazing company. I heard great things about them. They're the ones that set up tours and stays in outer space, right?"

Lisa nodded. "Yes, that's the one."

Janice was curious. "So, will you be assigned in outer space too?"

Lisa said, sheepishly. "Unfortunately, not as a new employee. They reserve outer space assignments to more experienced employees. Actually, not just experienced employees but only the very top performers. My biggest concern at the moment is how to make sure I do well on my job. I was hoping I could get some pointers from you."

Janice grinned and said, "We're just a small company not like SpaceZ Travel. My company is a very specialized digital marketing company. You may have heard of the term 'deep webbers'. That's what we do. We scour every nook and corner of the web . . . every digital information . . . to identify and analyze a company's web footprint. We then develop a plan for clients to enhance their brand and marketing efforts."

Janice took a sip of water and then continued. "The company's founders really wanted to leverage technology to help boost the Ps?"

"Huh?" Ben interrupted and looked at Ed, "Does this have anything to do with computer glitches?"

"To some extent, yes. We prevent glitches of any kind from happening. The Ps of course refer to *P*roductivity and *P*rofit. Like all firms, we care deeply about both. In fact, we have metrics in place to track our productivity and profit in real time."

Lisa waved her hand and an avatar appeared in the room and announced politely: "As of the current time, company productivity is up by 2 percent and profit up by 5 percent."

Janice thanked the avatar and continued. "Aside from the two Ps—Productivity and Profit—we also benchmark our performance with other companies based on three Ps—*P*eople, *P*lanet, and *P*rofit. We want to make sure we treat our stakeholders and environment well so that we have a sustainable enterprise."

Lisa was impressed that the small company implemented strategies more common to larger firms. She asked, "How are the needs of employees handled?"

"This may surprise you," Janice said. "We have an avatar that functions as the HR Manager. She's called CIAO— *C*areer *I*ntelligence and *A*utomation *O*fficer. She knows everything about every single employee—their history, their biometrics, and even their mood. All information is available in real time—performance, compensation, legal and regulatory, tax—you name it. All you have to do is say CIAO and she appears."

CIAO appeared and said, "Can I help you, Janice?"

"Sorry, CIAO. I don't need anything. I was just telling my family and friends about you. Thanks for showing up promptly."

"No problem. Hello everyone, and have a great day!" CIAO said, and disappeared.

Ben was amused. "Does that mean that CIAO knows exactly what's happening in the office all the time."

Janice nodded. "Yes, and more. Not only does she know what's happening, she analyzes what's happening and can predict and forecast human behavior."

Ed felt uncomfortable. "Do they know everything about guests as well?"

"Almost everything," Janice said.

"Doesn't it seem lopsided that machines know everything about humans and humans know little about them?" Ed asked.

"It does seem that way, but we try to make sure we keep some kind of balance. We want to make sure we retain an influential human touch in everything that we do. As an example, the company's co-founder Susan Smith manages most of the customer interface. She handles majority of stakeholder engagement, suggestions, customer interaction including complaints."

"Do you find it strange working with so many machines in the office?" Ben asked.

"Actually, I kind of like it as they do all the mundane stuff that I don't like. They do data gathering, number crunching, scenario planning, and connecting with the other bots. I can then focus on what I do best—planning, analyzing, and consulting with clients," Lisa answered.

Lisa followed the conversation intently. "How do you move up in the organization?"

"In my work, it's not so much about moving up. It's more about using resources within my control to make a real difference in the company. I am compensated for my level of productivity and contribution to the bottom line. Similar to many companies, our margins are tight. We rely on the efficiency and reliability of our team of humans and machines to succeed. Competition is tough and there are many operational challenges to worry about. We need to use our resources well and work efficiently as a team to survive."

"What operational challenges are common?"

"Oh, there as so many, Uncle Ed. One example is data integrity. We are web explorers and we find a lot of fake information on people that are false and inaccurate. Some of these are carried out as propaganda by dissenters, others by pranksters and scammers, and others—well, they are simply data tracking or computer error."

Ed felt vindicated. "That explains the recent computer glitch I experienced."

Lisa and Ben laughed as they recalled the mishap.

Janice continued. "Biases are also a problem. Sometimes, programmers include biases and prejudices in their work. This adversely impacts information accuracy."

"How did you learn so much about automation? Weren't you a marketing major in college?" Lisa asked.

"Well, we have some research collaboration with NYU, and over time they sponsored several technology-development training programs for all of us in the company. And you know what, because there's so much new technology every day, we have 15 minutes of technology-training updates every day."

Ed was surprised. "Every day?"

"Yes, it has become part of our work. Learning is work, and at this point in time—the two are indistinguishable. The more I can use what I learn immediately, the more relevant it is to me, and the better contribution I can make to the company."

Ed came across an idea. "I need to get into one of those university bite-size technology training to get up to speed."

"Me too," Lisa and Ben chimed in together.

"I think the fact that I diligently viewed those bite-size tech lessons, really helped me do well and stand out in my job."

The trio thanked Janice and prepared to leave. As they stepped out of the room, an avatar appeared in the corner and said, "Hello Janice, with this meeting, your personal productivity metrics is down by 3 percent. However, your work earlier in the day increased company profit metrics by 7 percent. Good job!"

They all laughed.

Right Turn Lesson # 6

Companies will be very focused on profitability and productivity enhancement. Employees need to optimize resource usage to truly stand out in the organization.

Technology Roadmap

The Internet of Things (IoT) refers to the integration of objects with sensors, software, and other technologies in order that data can be collected and analyzed using the Internet. According to a report from Transforma Insights, the global IoT market will grow to over $24 billion in 2030 and will generate $1.5 trillion in revenue. Industries that will benefit from IoT include manufacturing, healthcare, agriculture, hospitality, retail, finance, transportation, automobile industry, energy, and smart homes and buildings among many others. The Transforma Insights website offers useful industry information on this technology.

For more information go to the epilogue.

8

VIRTUAL CALL

Ben Johnson planned to meet up with Michael James his former co-worker at his company's headquarters in New Jersey. He is a 33-year-old Black man who's making waves with his ideas, business, and personal savvy at the headquarters. They were supposed to meet up in his office, but a last-minute trip came up and he offered to do a virtual call instead.

This was the message exchange in their handheld remote systems (HRS):

Michael: Ben a last-minute trip came up. Can we do a holo call?

Ben: Sure, when can you do it?

Michael: In 15 minutes. Does that work?

Ben: Yes, I appreciate your taking the time.

Michael: It's a pleasure. See you in 15 minutes.

The two men typed in the appointment in the calendar in their HRS, known in the earlier days' mobile phones. Ben was amused that the old version of the device was actually a phone. Who uses that nowadays? With HRS, information appears on a virtual display in front of the device. On voice command or according to program, the hologram of any person in the world—actually even from someone in outer space—will pop up instantly.

At the designated time, Michael's virtual image popped up:

"Ben, it's nice meeting you today. Sorry, we could not meet in person but you sure look good," Michael said.

"Well, holograms make me look 10 pounds lighter than I am."

"In my case, I programmed it to add 15 pounds so I look stronger. How do you like my programmed accent? I'm using a slight British accent on my hologram."

"Very cool. I almost didn't recognize you."

Michael smiled, then continued. "What can I help you with, Ben?"

Ben's disposition changed. "You know I love the company and I am working really hard. However, I haven't gotten a promotion in four years. I got a small raise and some bonuses. But, they just brought in a new manager and I thought I should have gotten that role."

Michael felt sorry for his friend. "Hold on, let me check on the E5 system."

Ben nodded. "Yes, the infamous E5—*E*mployee, *E*xperience, *E*ngagement, and *E*nhancement *E*cosystem. I get frequent messages from it on my benefits, training needs assessment, and upskilling progress. It does an awesome job—very data driven and analytical.

"Well, at the headquarters some of us have access to portions of it. In my case, I'd be able to see job trends, upskilling programs, future organizational needs and forecasts, and even succession plans. Let me take a quick peek."

Michael read through the virtual file and continued. "It's showing me you are doing great at work. But, it doesn't show you volunteering or participating in much else that goes on in the company. And, you don't seem to have made an impression with our senior leaders. Your scores there are pretty low. Sorry."

Ben was confused. "Pretty low? Volunteering? I thought I had to focus solely on delivering my work?"

"Ben, work is paramount, however, you have to at least participate in the many Employee Resource Groups (ERGs), community or company activities that we sponsor. Have you not participated in any?" Michael asked.

Ben pondered for a minute. "I believe I attended a couple of those."

"Did you ever volunteer to lead any projects?"

"No, not really," Ben said.

Michael continued reading a virtual file, and said, "How do you think your other two managers got visible to senior management? I can't read their history to you, but do you recall them participating in events or company activities before they became managers?"

Ben gave the matter some thought. "Now that you bring it up, I always wondered why they were so into the community projects. I know they invited me to participate several times and I declined. I had deadlines to meet to address the needs of customers."

"Work and customers is what keeps the company growing, but, many of the other things that go on in the company keep you visible to the right people," Michael stated. "Let me ask you a question. How many people do you think there are at your level in the organization? Few? A lot?"

"A lot," Ben answered, wondering where his friend was going with this.

Michael continued. "And, how do you think senior leaders in our organization remember who you are or even recognize your name, if you don't give them a chance or way to know you?"

Ben thought to himself. "I might have miscalculated the importance of these seemingly innocuous activities. Never realized they were that important."

"I will ask you one more question, okay? Have you ever proactively volunteered to do something for your manager or their manager that they had spoken passionately about?" Michael asked.

"No, not really," Ben said sheepishly.

"My dear friend, from day one when we worked together you were a brilliant worker. However, an organization is much more complex than just results and getting work done. The robots, avatars, technicians can do much of that. How do you become indispensable to the other humans that lead the organization? When your name comes up, do people only remember the work you do or all the other projects, initiatives, and activities you participated with them?"

Ben felt like a ton of bricks just fell on him. "This is quite a wake-up call. I never knew it was that important."

"It is. If you want a career and career progression, you have to find balance. Be technically strong, but also know how to engage and endear yourself to individuals both up and down the organization. Are you open to doing that?"

"Sure, yes of course."

"I have one personal advice, one that worked very well for me. We face a lot of demands in our work. There's a lot of pressure. We often lose sight of what we really need to do to grow and develop. Two years ago, I took a mini-sabbatical. I took a month off to review my career and assess what I really need to do to find the best version of myself. This is what I found out. The best job for you is the one that you create. Meaning, leverage your best abilities and personal passion to excel in the job. Some call this job crafting. And, the very best way to implement job crafting is to create your Personal Career Development Plan. Don't let other people decide your career. Take control of it."

Ben was inspired by his friend's passion for his career and strategic thinking. "How do you create a Personal Career Development Plan?"

"It's actually quite simple. You assess your present skills, then your aspirations, then identify what you need to do to bridge the gap from where you are now to where you want to go. I'm not sure you're aware, there's actually a template in the E5 that shows how you can create your Personal Career Development Plan. It's confidential, and it's for your own personal use. E5 tracks it and provides you with a progress report based on the milestones you've achieved. It has helped me a lot."

Ben was enthusiastic. "I will sure create one."

"I need to go. But, if you like we can have a virtual call in six months to discuss your progress."

"That would be great. Thank you so much, Michael."

"You're most welcome. If we do this right, maybe you can get assigned here in the headquarters in a year or two."

"That is what I'm really hoping for, since my girlfriend Lisa will be working in New York."

"Great," Michael said. "Do send my very best to Lisa. And, good luck!

Ben got off the call and was truly grateful for the advice he received. He learned a lot from the brief call. He made a note to share what he learned with Ed and Lisa. The insights would be of help to both of them—actually also to all employees around the world.

Right Turn Lesson # 7

Employees need to take charge of their own destiny, and design their own personal development journey through a Personal Career Development Plan.

Technology Roadmap

5G refers to the fifth-generation standard for technology deployed by cellular phone companies allowing increased bandwidth and faster download speeds. The global 5G devices market is expected to exceed $45 billion by 2030. Industries that will benefit from this technology include manufacturing, energy, agriculture, healthcare, financial services, insurance, retail, media and entertainment, transportation and hospitality among many others. A McKinsey Report titled, "The 5G Era" available over the web is a useful resource on this technology.

For more information go to the epilogue.

9

SpaceZ

Lisa looked up at the tall building where SpaceZ Travel Group headquarters and the cybersecurity team were located. She was there a little early, as she was so excited to start and meet her new boss Sandra Lee, Head of Global Cybersecurity.

Sandra graciously welcomed Lisa. "It is so nice to finally meet you in person."

Lisa's elation was evident. "I am so excited to be here."

"Thank you for filling up all the documentation and onboarding sessions before you arrived," Sandra said.

"The system was really intuitive and engaging. I did most of my medical check-up as well."

"You do know you are one of the special few who were shortlisted to work at our Company Support Center (CSC). Most of our staff are spread around the country and the world. We also have 53 other country or regional CSC office locations to support our customers," Sandra stated.

Lisa nodded. "Yes, I remember that from the onboarding session. In fact, I was able to speak to three staffers and even sat in on a customer call as part of that plan. It provided me with an excellent perspective on what we do here."

Sandra was curious. "So what where your main takeaways from onboarding?"

Lisa gave it some thought and replied. "Well Sandra, I took away three key ideas that stood out as being most important. First, we take care of our family both at home and at work so that we are free to delight our customers. That sets up the second takeaway, which is a focus on productivity and efficiency in all aspects of our operations so that we delight our stakeholders. Third, we engage, collaborate with, and anticipate what our customers need and deliver that to them."

Sandra was impressed. "That was quite insightful. I would add that we make sure we leverage emerging technology to always stay ahead of the competition."

Lisa smiled. "Yes, I do remember that."

Sandra reciprocated with a wide grin. "That's great. I want to share all the things you will notice around here that help us with efficiency. First, our CWO (Chief Workforce Officer), Anil Moorthy, has assigned a robo-assistant, Nancy, to you. You will meet Anil at the end of our session. Nancy will double up as your avatar and attend meetings on your behalf so that you can literally be in two places at one time. It will get a little bit getting used to as she may be asking you for your answers in your earpiece, and you will respond via your company issued HRS. You will learn after a while that she knows how you will tend to respond. The avatar will only ask for your inputs on important issues."

Nancy appeared from the corner of the room. She looked exactly like Lisa.

Nancy said warmly. "Welcome on board Lisa—I am glad to be of assistance to you."

Lisa was amazed. "Great to meet you, Nancy. When I see you, I feel like I'm looking at my twin."

"I am technically your twin," Nancy said. "The digital version."

Sandra was pleased with how everything was progressing. "Nancy will take you on a tour of the office and your work station after our meeting."

"That would be excellent. Thank you so much," Lisa said, with much gratitude.

"Oh, I almost forgot. I'd like to point out that at SpaceZ Travel we have Chief Happiness Officers to ensure our employees are feeling at their physiological best so that they can contribute at the highest level and not be unduly stressed. They take care of your preventative health and ensure you are happy and if you need help with anything. You can identify them by their bright yellow outfits."

"Yes, I met one during onboarding and she helped with planning my trip here."

"Perfect," Sandra replied. "They are available for you 24/7."

Sandra pulled out her HRS and a hologram appeared. "Here's a short welcome message from our CEO Mark Cartwright."

The hologram spoke: "Good morning, Lisa, welcome to SpaceZ Travel. I am really glad you joined our team. I hope you have had a pleasant experience with onboarding and know you are special because you have been picked to work at the headquarters. I believe I have a one-on-one scheduled with you already and your assistant will confirm that with you. I am always looking for forward-thinking, creative, and innovative staff. This is the only way to leverage all the resources we have here at SpaceZ and produce even better products and services for our customers. As Sandra will tell you, that's how we get to the pinnacle of success—with people like you, and I know your ability and capacity to do marvelous work. I am looking forward to meeting you soon in person. Again, welcome to SpaceZ Travel."

Lisa was touched and impressed. "Wow, did he make that message, especially for me?"

"Yes—in your case, because you are new here at NY CSC. We know that each employee has the potential to change the company and turn it around. We are very proud of each of our new hires."

Lisa beamed with pride.

Sandra continued. "We also actively reward excellent performance. As Mark mentioned, we have an award committee here at SpaceZ Travel that constantly reviews and evaluates work results, collaborative skills, and innovative contributions. You could be chosen as a "Pinnacle Ace."

There are only five Pinnacle Aces chosen in a year. It's a very big deal because not only do you get the award from Mark, but you also join him on an outer space trip using one of our "Transporters."

Lisa was dumbfounded. "Oh, my gosh."

Sandra continued. "The award ceremony is a major event in our company. You could be one of our winners next year. Some new hires do get the award because of the fresh perspective provided and their innovative ideas. Some of the winners created new products, others implemented new work systems, yet others took customer relationships to a new level. There are many pathways toward getting the Pinnacle Ace Award. I know this is a lot to throw at you at once. Why don't you first take the tour of the office and settle into your work station. I will see you in the afternoon, and we will lay out your work goals for the quarter and the year. I will provide you with pointers on the best way to succeed here at SpaceZ Travel. See you at 1.00 pm. Anil will join us in the afternoon meeting. I know he'd love to meet you."

Nancy approached Lisa from the side. "I am so glad to be your assistant, Lisa. Let's go take a tour of the office. Your work station is through the hallway and on the next *right*.

Right Turn Lesson # 8

Employees need to be game–changers and innovators, leveraging talent and resources to make a difference in the company and achieve the pinnacle of success.

Technology Roadmap

Biometrics are measurements and calculations of the human body and characteristics presently used alongside computers for identification and control purposes. According to a Grace Market Data (GMD) research report, the global biometrics as a service market will exceed $10 billion by 2030. Industries that would benefit from this technology include food and beverage, hospitality, retail, healthcare, education, automotive, air travel and migration, financial services and banking, and law enforcement among others. A report by the Biometrics Research Group titled "Mobile Biometrics Market Analysis—Biometric Update" available over the web offers useful information on this technology.

For more information go to the epilogue.

10

GETTING IT RIGHT

It had been a hectic but significant week for Ed, Lisa, and Ben. Since it was a Saturday morning, they decided to visit Central Park. They sat on a park bench, and took sight of the greenery and people amidst one of the biggest cities in the world.

Ed gazed across the pond and broke his silence. "I am really glad I came on this trip, Lisa."

Lisa was touched. "Thanks, Dad, it meant so much to me."

"I learned a few things that I don't think I would have if I had stayed in Decatur," Ed said pensively. "First, I realized everyone needs to upgrade their skills and be life-long learners. For me, it is largely about keeping current and exploring something new. It's almost a must these days as competition is tough, and everyone is trying to differentiate themselves and add compelling value to the company."

Ben added. "I definitely see that Ed. It was a wake-up call to see how technology can be put to great use even in government."

Ed agreed. "That's right, Ben, and you know there will be more gadgets and tools that will emerge. We just need to embrace them more quickly."

Lisa watched a young mother pass by with a baby, riding an autonomous stroller. She chimed in. "Imagine the world that child will grow up in!"

Lisa continued. "There will be machines and robots at work, at home, and even in the park."

They cast glances at several Nanny-bots that were assisting families with their children. There were also robo-vendors passing out ice cream to the families.

"We will need to learn to work with them symbiotically," Lisa said.

Ben concurred. "That is so true, Lisa. I am glad you see that right from the start of your career journey. Emerging technologies need not be daunting to us at work. We need to change our attitude, overcome our insecurities, and just take gradual steps to get comfortable with it."

Ben had an insight and shared it. "The biggest lesson is, everyone needs to take charge of their own destiny, their personal development and build a plan for themselves. Just take the initiative and do it."

Lisa nodded. "I know I am going to do that as soon as I can. Otherwise, I will get caught up on focusing on profitability and productivity for the company and forget about myself. I am not going to miss that one. It's the key to my personal growth and happiness. Thanks, Ben, for reminding me."

Ben smiled. "You're welcome. We all need a little reminding once in a while. Actually, in my case, it happened to be a kick in the behind."

The trio laughed.

Lisa was inspired and felt optimistic about the future. "My company's CEO mentioned that they are looking at all of us to help by being game-changers and innovators for our company and all our stakeholders. We need to do well for ourselves, our company, our customers, and our community. With the lessons I learned from our trip to New York, I am confident I can make a real difference in the company and society, perhaps even reach the pinnacle of success."

Ed looked at Lisa proudly. "I'm sure you'll do an amazing job. You have a long and bright future ahead of you. It looks like we took the right *right* turns on our way here."

Lisa was enthusiastic. "I can't wait for the next *right*."

Ed's HRS buzzed and the virtual image reminded him it was time to head back to Decatur.

Ed gave Lisa and Ben a big hug. "I'll miss you both. I have to head back and get started on my new venture with Cindy and Jim. It looks like we already have two clients and we haven't even started."

Lisa watched Ed as he prepared to leave. She felt sad to see him go, but was also very pleased that he found a new career and meaning in life. "Do stay in touch," she said.

Ed embraced and kissed her. "I certainly will. Do take care, dearie."

Ed crossed the street and stopped. He briefly deliberated on whether to proceed left or right turn. "What the heck?" he thought. "Why would I even doubt this?" He promptly took the *right* path.

Lisa and Ben waived at Ed from a distance.

They held hands and walked in the park pondering their future together.

Ben made plans to join Lisa in New York the following year. He uncovered a pathway toward a promotion in his firm. He can get assigned in the corporate headquarters in a year if he accomplished his goals. He felt more determined than he's ever been in his life. He had to make significant changes and sacrifices, but his prospects looked good.

Much had changed in the past few days. Lisa and Ben started off with self-doubt and frustration and uncovered newfound joy and inspiration. They shared a thought. "Watch out New York, here we come!"

As the sun started to set in the horizon, they took the *right* steps toward their new home.

EPILOGUE

The story offered key insights that would be helpful for executives at different career stages within a growingly digital world.

Eight lessons were featured to aid in one's success in a growingly technology-driven corporate environment.

Eight Strategies to a Successful Personal Developmental Journey

Lesson 1	Employees need to upgrade their skills and pursue lifelong learning to keep their jobs.
Lesson 2	Competition will be tough, employees need to differentiate their skills and focus on where they can truly add value.
Lesson 3	Many new technological gadgets and tools will emerge, employees need to learn to embrace technology quickly.
Lesson 4	There will be machines and robots in the workplace, employees need to learn to work hand in hand with machines and practice symbiotic computing.
Lesson 5	Emerging technologies will be daunting to many, employees need to overcome technological insecurity and fear by changing their attitude and taking gradual steps toward progress.
Lesson 6	Companies will be very focused on profitability and productivity enhancement, employees need to optimize resource usage to truly stand out in the organization.

Lesson 7	Employees need to take charge of their own destiny, and design their own personal development journey through a Personal Career Development Plan.
Lesson 8	Employees need to be game-changers and innovators, leveraging talent and resources to make a difference in the company and achieve the pinnacle of success.

In analyzing this development journey, it is evident that the employee's growth would come in different stages. Depending on which stage an employee is at, certain developmental skill sets would need to be emphasized.

Four Stages of a Professional Development Journey

STAGE 1—SKILL UPGRADE

Employees need to upgrade their skills and pursue lifelong learning to keep their jobs.

Competition will be tough, employees need to differentiate their skills and focus on where they can truly add value.

STAGE 2—TECHNOLOGY ASSIMILATION

Many new technological gadgets and tools will emerge, employees need to learn to embrace technology quickly.

There will be machines and robots in the workplace, employees need to learn to work hand in hand with machines and practice symbiotic computing.

STAGE 3—ATTITUDINAL CHANGE

Emerging technologies will be daunting to many, employees need to overcome technological insecurity and fear by changing their attitude and taking gradual steps toward progress.

Companies will be very focused on profitability and productivity enhancement, employees need to optimize resource usage to truly stand out in the organization.

STAGE 4—RESOURCE OPTIMIZATION

Employees need to take charge of their own destiny, and design their own personal development journey through a Personal Career Development Plan.

Employees need to be game-changers and innovators, leveraging talent and resources to make a difference in the company and achieve the pinnacle of success.

When embarking on a career growth path, employees need to carefully and strategically weigh upon the skills they need to improve on, technology they need to learn, attitudes they need to change, and resources they need to use to accomplish their goals. The technology roadmaps featured throughout the book underscores the significant role key technologies will play in the organizations of the future.

Employees are at different stages of development and should consider pursuing advancement appropriate to the stage they are in.

As mentioned, the four stages to a professional development journey are: **S**kill Upgrade, **T**echnology Assimilation, **A**ttitudinal Change, and **R**esource Optimization. Coincidentally, the acronym is **STAR**. When lost, follow the **STAR**.

A good development journey requires an early personal assessment so that proper planning can be made. The following guide questions can be helpful in assessing developmental needs.

Professional Journey Development Assessment Questionnaire

Skill Upgrade	What skills do I need to upgrade to help me do a better job? How can I leverage these skills to truly differentiate myself and make a valuable contribution to my organization? What can I do to continually learn and grow and make learning a habit?
Technology Assimilation	What are the latest emerging technologies out there and how can I learn about them? What can I do to gain cutting-edge knowledge in areas such as Artificial Intelligence, Automation, Internet of Things, and Augmented Reality? How can I improve myself in symbiotic computing?
Attitudinal Change	What are my fears and apprehensions about technology? Why do these fears exist? What can I do to allay these fears and concerns? How can I transform these fears into a positive mindset and action plan? What gradual steps can I take toward improvement? How can I better focus on productivity and profitability?
Resource Optimization	What are my professional and life goals, and how do I integrate them in a Personal Career Development Plan? What resources do I need to accomplish my goals? What steps can I take to make a significant difference in my organization?

A successful voyage starts with asking the right questions, educating oneself, planning ahead, and implementing set goals methodically. It's about knowing exactly where you want to go and how to get there. In one's career, it's about taking the next right step.

Staying abreast with current thinking on the future of work and emerging technologies can be helpful.

BIBLIOGRAPHY

Books and Journals

Baldwin, Richard. *The Globotics Upheaval: Globalization, Robotics and the Future of Work*. UK: Oxford University Press, February 8, 2019.

Diamandis, Peter, and Steven Kotler. *The Future Is Faster Than You Think: How Converging Technologies Are Transforming Business, Industries and Our Lives*. New York City: Simon & Schuster, January 28, 2020.

Ebelle-Ebanda, A., and G. Newman. "Organizational Network Analytics and the Future of Work." *Workforce Solutions Review* 9, no. 2 (2018): 13–17. Accessed September 27, 2020. http://mulinutil1.millikin.edu:2060/login.aspx?direct=true&db=bsh&AN=132838765&site=ehost-live&scope=site.

G20 Emphasizes Training in Skills for Challenges Posed by the Future of Work. *International Trade Forum* no. 3 (2018): 7. Accessed September 27, 2020. http://mulinutil1.millikin.edu:2060/login.aspx?direct=true&db=bsh&AN=133941908&site=ehost-live&scope=site.

Griswold, D. "The Once and Future Worker: A Vision for the Renewal of Work in America." *CATO Journal* 40, no. 1 (2020): 240–43. Accessed September 27, 2020. https://www.cato.org/cato-journal/winter-2020/once-future-worker-vision-renewal-work-america-oren-cass?queryID=86c52ab3f61d9314914eee388cd39b8a.

Morgan, Jacob. *The Future of Work: Attract New Talent, Build Better Leaders, and Create a Competitive Organization*. New Jersey: Wiley, August 25, 2014.

SAKO, M. "Artificial Intelligence and the Future of Professional Work: Considering the Implications of the Influence of

Artificial Intelligence Given Previous Industrial Revolutions." *Communications of the ACM [s. l.]* 63, no. 4 (2020): 25–27.

Smith, E. "Apprenticeships and 'Future Work': Are We Ready?" *International Journal of Training & Development* 23, no. 1 (2019): 69–88. doi:10.1111/ijtd.12145.

Smith, Scott, and Madeline Ashby. *How to Future: Leading and Sense-Making In an Age of Hyperchange.* London: Kogan Page, September 29, 2020.

Tasha Hyacinth, Brigette. *Leading the Workforce of the Future: Inspiring a Mindset of Passion, Innovation and Growth.* MBA Carribean Organization, February 14, 2020.

West, Darrell M. *The Future of Work: Robots, AI and Automation.* Washington, DC: Brookings Institution Press, May 15, 2018.

Educational Videos

The future of work: AILA and Google https://www.youtube.com/watch?v=n7VoVMV375U.

The future of work: A VICE news special report https://www.youtube.com/watch?v=_iaKHeCKcq4.

The future of work: Is your job safe? https://www.youtube.com/watch?v=gUc5oN_ffRo.

The future of work: Robots, AI and automation https://www.youtube.com/watch?v=YjVW4dD88hk.

The future of work: What's at stake? https://www.youtube.com/watch?v=6Xon5pW2Ov0.

Online Resources

ATOS Report on the Future of Work https://atos.net/wp-content/uploads/2017/09/atos-future-of-work-trends-report.pdf.

BSR Report—How business can build a future of work that works for women https://www.bsr.org/reports/BSR-WomenDeliver-Future-of-Work-for-Women-Framework.pdf.

Cognizant Report on 21 Jobs of the Future https://www.cognizant.com/whitepapers/21-jobs-of-the-future-a-guide-to-getting-and-staying-employed-over-the-next-10-years-codex3049.pdf.

Deloitte Report on What is the Future of Work https://www2.deloitte.com/content/dam/Deloitte/nl/Documents/humancapital/deloitte-nl-hc-what-is-the-future-of-work.pdf.

IMF Report on the Future of Work—Measurement and Policy Challenges https://www.imf.org/external/np/g20/pdf/2018/071818a.pdf.

Jesus College Cambridge, KPMG and Harvey Nash—The Future of Work Report https://assets.kpmg/content/dam/kpmg/fr/pdf/2017/05/fr-Future-Of-Work-report.pdf.

McKinsey & Company Report on the Future of Work https://www.mckinsey.com/featured-insights/future-of-work/the-future-of-work-in-america-people-and-places-today-and-tomorrow.

NESTA Report—The future of skills employment in 2030 https://media.nesta.org.uk/documents/the_future_of_skills_employment_in_2030_0.pdf.

OECD Report on the Future of Work and Skills https://www.oecd.org/els/emp/wcms_556984.pdf.

Pew Research Center Report on the Future of Work in the Automated Workplace https://www.pewsocialtrends.org/2019/03/21/the-future-of-work-in-the-automated-workplace/.

PWC Report—The way we work in 2025 and beyond https://www.pwc.ch/en/publications/2017/the-way-we-work-hr-today_pwc-en_2017.pdf.

PWC Report on the Workforce of the Future https://www.pwc.com/gx/en/services/people-organisation/publications/workforce-of-the-future.html.

UKCES Report on the Future of Work https://assets.publishing.service.gov.uk/government/uploads/system/uploads/attachment_data/file/303335/the_future_of_work_key_findings_edit.pdf. Washington Workforce Board—The Future of Work Task Force 2019 Policy Report https://www.wtb.wa.gov/wp-content/uploads/2019/12/Future-of-Work-2019-Final-Report.pdf.

Workhuman Analytics Research Institute Survey—The Future of Work is Human https://www.workhuman.com/press-releases/White_Paper_The_Future_of_Work_is_Human.pdf.

World Economic Report on the Future of Jobs http://www3.weforum.org/docs/WEF_Future_of_Jobs.pdf.

Podcasts

a16Z (Andreesen-Horowitz)
Back to Work
Exponent (Ben Thompson and James Allworth)
Flash Forward
Future of Work (Jacob Morgan)
Future Thinkers
HBS Managing the Future of Work
IDEO Futures
Innovation Hub
IT Visionaries
Mind and Machine
Review the Future
Technotopia
ThinkFuture by HelloFuture
WSJ's The Future of Everything

Social Influencers

Listed by Lisa Ardill in a Silicon Republic article published on August 26, 2020.
Abby Langtry
Alan Lepofsky
Alex Ferreira
Ali Fazal
Ann Roddy
Chris Herd
Dave Anderson
Eva Sage-Gavin
James Milligan
Jim Stanford
Kirsti Lonka
Sarah Cunningham
Sarah Winton
Sheree Atcheson
Soraya Darabi
Tim Salau

Technology Readiness Training and Executive Development

The authors offer several in-house or virtual program options:

- Keynotes
- Virtual Presentations
- Roundtable Discussion with Technology Experts
- Fireside Chat with a Technology Leader
- Technology Introduction Programs for Students
- Technology Introduction Programs for Employees
- Brainstorming Session on Technology and Strategy
- Podcast/Videocast

For more information, visit the website: https://www.winninginthe workworld.com/thenextrightmove/

ABOUT THE AUTHORS

J. Mark Munoz is a tenured Full Professor of Management and International Business at Millikin University in Illinois, and a former Visiting Fellow at the Kennedy School of Government at Harvard University. He is a recipient of several awards including four Best Research Paper Awards, a Literary Award, two International Book Awards, and the ACBSP Teaching Excellence Award among others. He was recognized by the Academy of Global Business Advancement as the 2016 Distinguished Business Dean and recognized for Global Academic Excellence by Amity/IEEE in 2019. Aside from top-tier journal publications, he has authored/edited/co-edited over twenty books including, *Contemporary Microenterprises: Concepts and Cases, Handbook on the Geopolitics of Business, Hispanic-Latino Entrepreneurship, African American Entrepreneurs, Managerial Forensics, Advances in Geoeconomics, Business Strategies in an AI Economy, The Handbook of Artificial Intelligence and Robotic Process Automation: Policy and Government Applications, The Economics of Cryptocurrencies*, and *Global Business Intelligence*. He directs consulting projects worldwide in the areas of strategy formulation, international marketing, and business development.

Stephen Krempl Stephen Krempl is an International Speaker, Facilitator, Best-Selling Author, and Business Communication Coach. He has helped thousands of leaders in corporations and students in over thirty countries become more visible to senior management. He created the Global Executive Mindset (GEM) program that teaches high potential future leaders to be more visible in their organizations. This program, offered both as in-house workshops and as an online program has benefited numerous individuals and organizations globally. Clients include Applied Materials, BNP Paribas, BASF, VISA, Global Foundries, Schnieder Electric, DBS, OCBC, National Université of Singapore, Washington State Univerisity, Human Capital Leadership Institute, SSIA.

Stephen has also extended the GEM message to students, through an online program called Winning in the Work World™ (W3 Online), to prepare them as they step into the work world. Stephen's professional career spans over 25 years in Fortune 500 companies. He played pivotal roles as Chief Learning Officer of Starbucks Coffee Company. At YUM Brands, he was Vice President of YUM University & Global Learning, and senior positions at PepsiCo Restaurants International and Motorola. He is also the author of five books, including his latest *The 5% Zone: Visibility Strategies that Get You Noticed and Rewarded in any Organization*. His experience has given him valuable insights into what employers are looking for and how executives can stand out in their organizations, even in an increasingly competitive global marketplace.

Printed in the USA
CPSIA information can be obtained
at www.ICGtesting.com
LVHW041245070824
787596LV00002B/21